Always with Me

by Susie Poole

Authentic

'a time to be loved'

This edition copyright © 2022 Authentic Media Limited
Text and illustrations copyright © 2002 and 1996 Susie Poole
The moral right of Susie Poole to be identified as the author
and illustrator of this work has been asserted.

First published 1996 by Nelson Word Limited
This revised omnibus edition first published 2022
by Authentic Media Limited, PO Box 6326, Bletchley,
Milton Keynes, MK1 9GG. authenticmedia.co.uk

10 9 8 7 6 5 4 3 2 1

ISBN 978 1 78893 147 2

All rights reserved

Printed in Great Britain by Bell and Bain, Glasgow

A Time For Everything

Based on Ecclesiastes 3, The Bible

Life is wonderful
and there is a time
for everything.

Happy times
when we say

       hello...

A time to be muddy and squelchy.

A time to be **clean and soapy.**

A time for summer and keeping

and wrapping up warm.

And time to be really noisy!!

A time to love.

And a time to be loved.

A time to

wake up.

There is a time for everything.

'Because this does me good.'

Whatever is Lovely

Based on Philippians 4, verses 8 & 9, The Bible

There are **things** that make me feel...

And **things** that make me **sad.**

And sometimes life seems so

unfair!

But I **won't worry**
about these things.
I'll **talk to God**
and he'll help me.

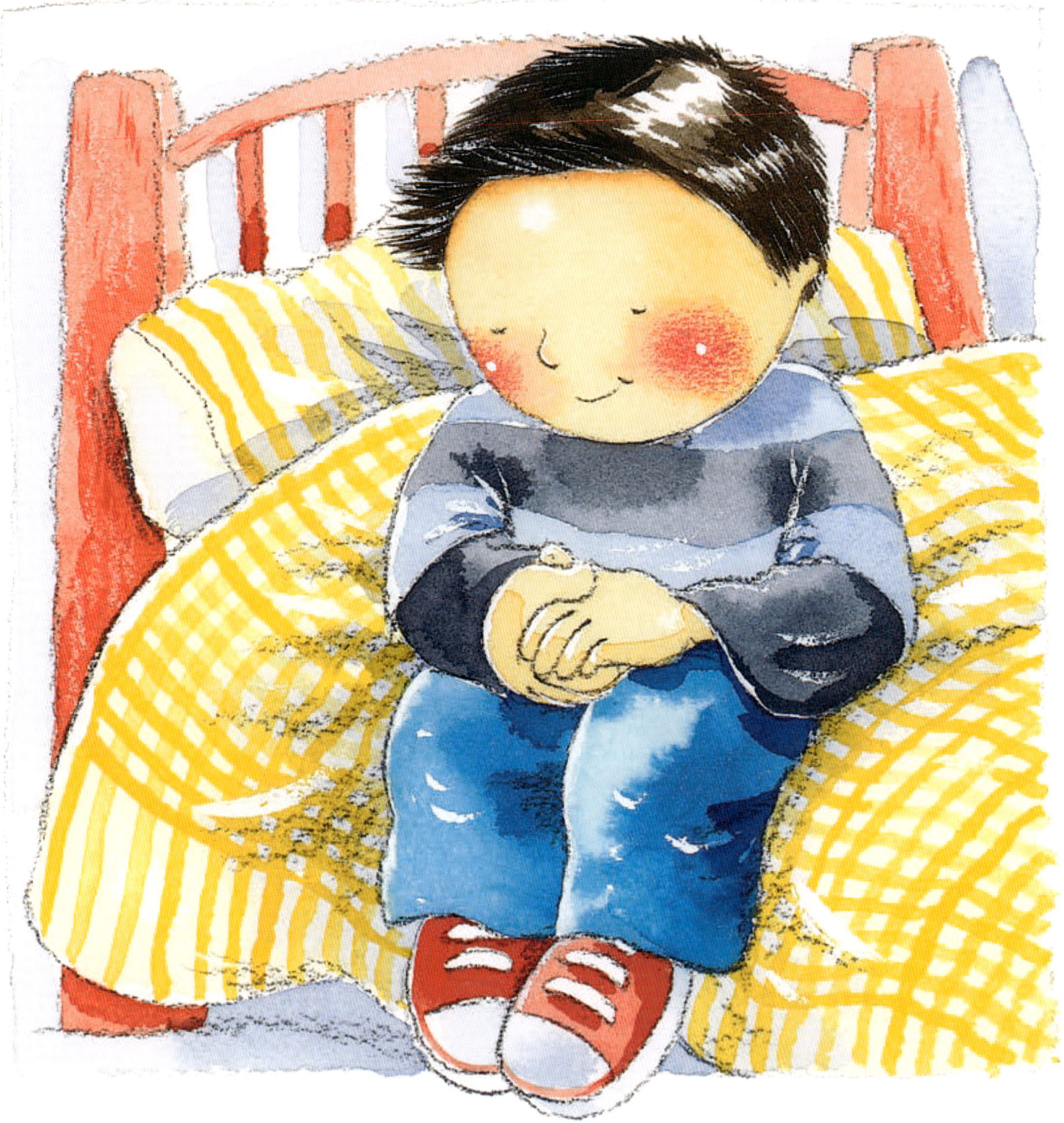

And then...

I'll think about **whatever is lovely.**

I'll think about things that are... amazing.

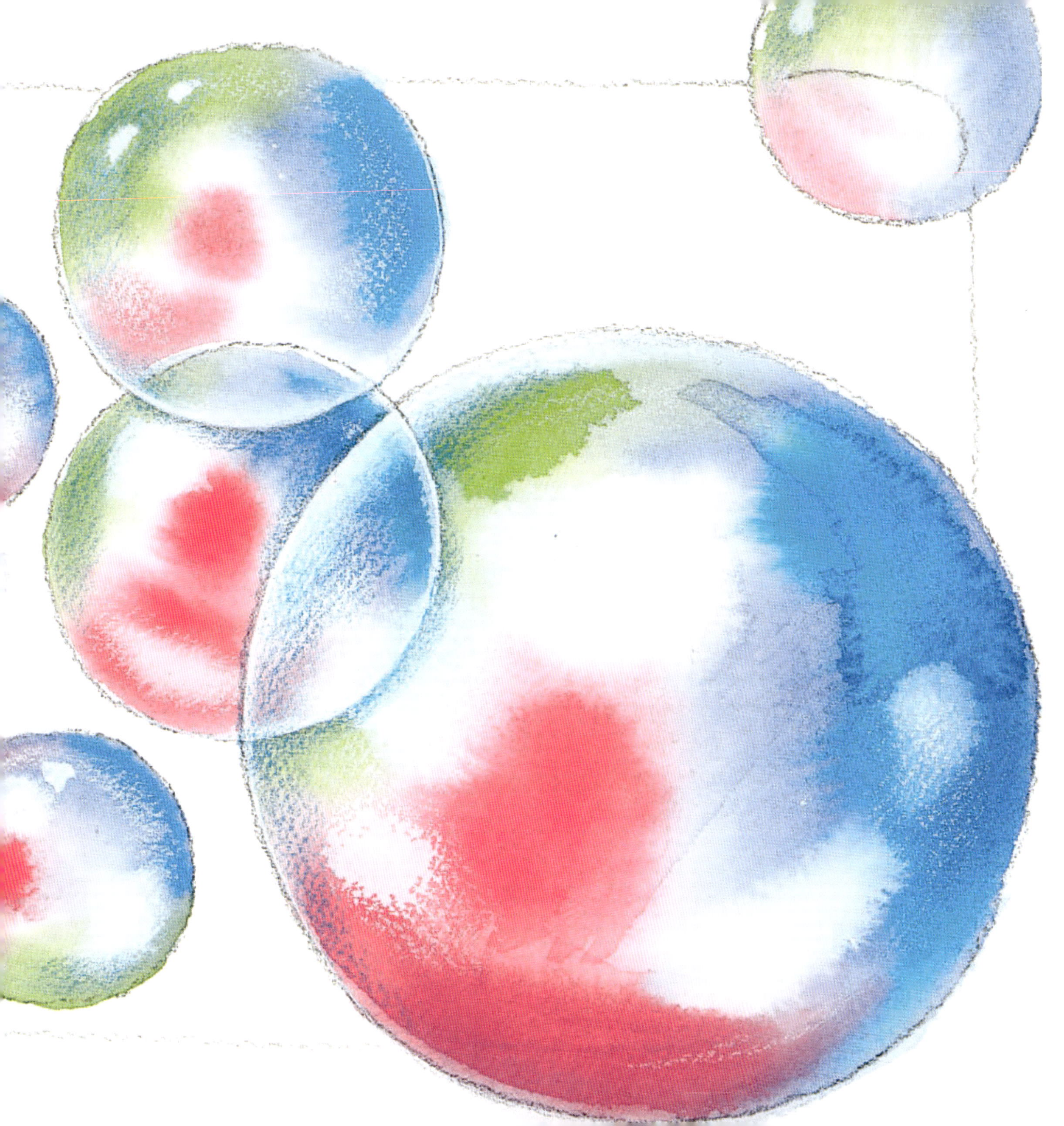

Things very **great.**

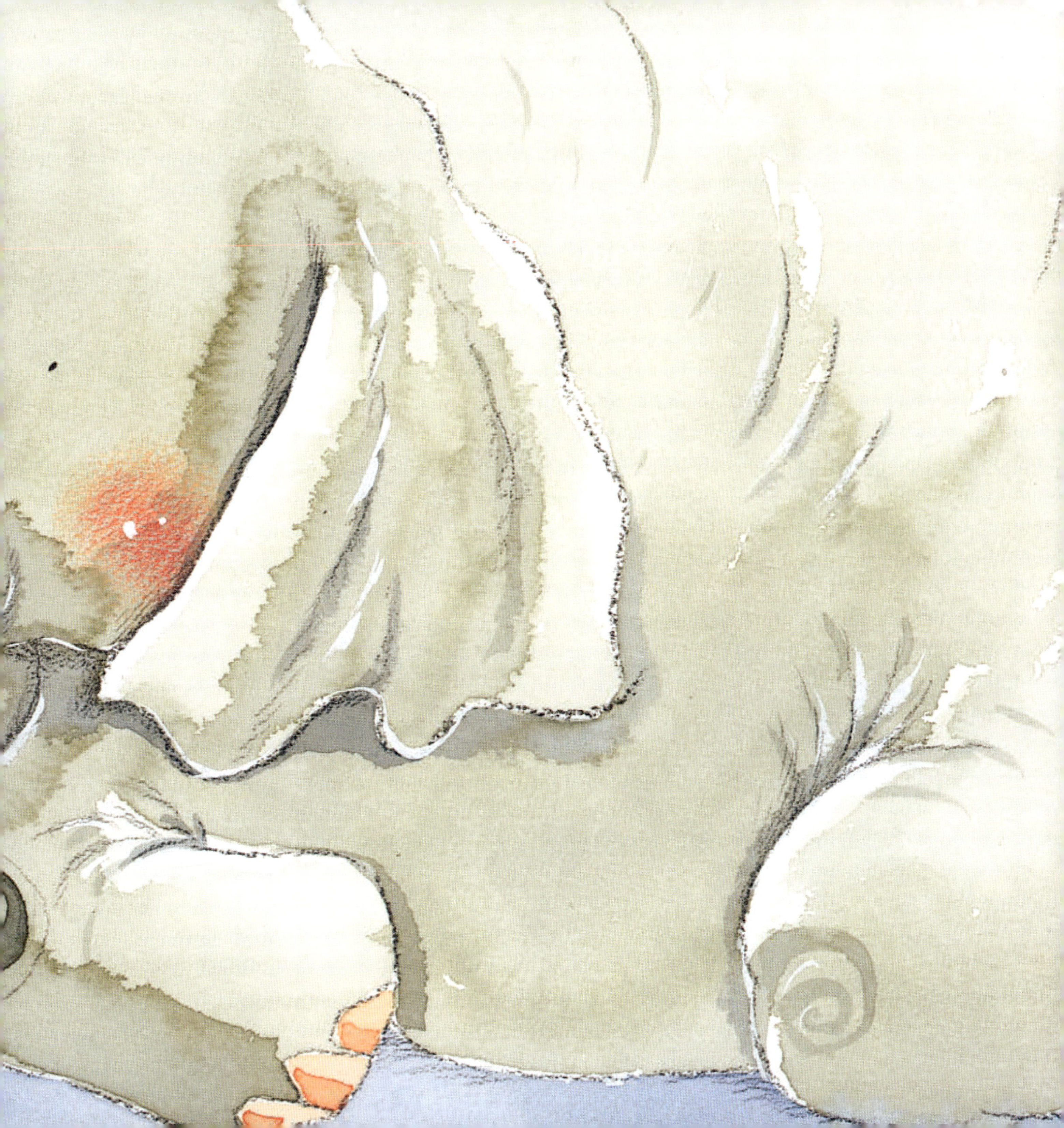

Things very...

small.

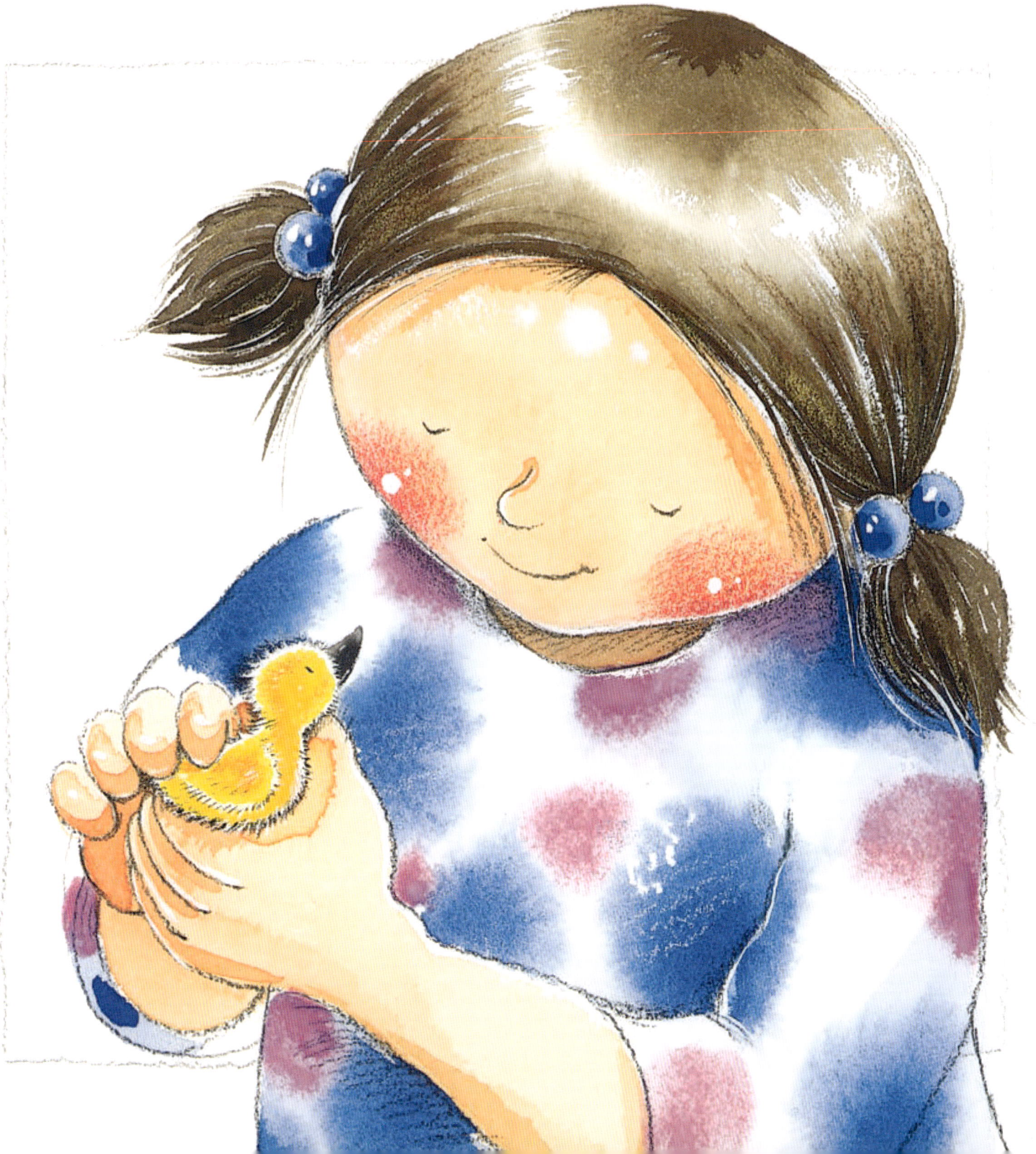

I'll think about someone who is kind.

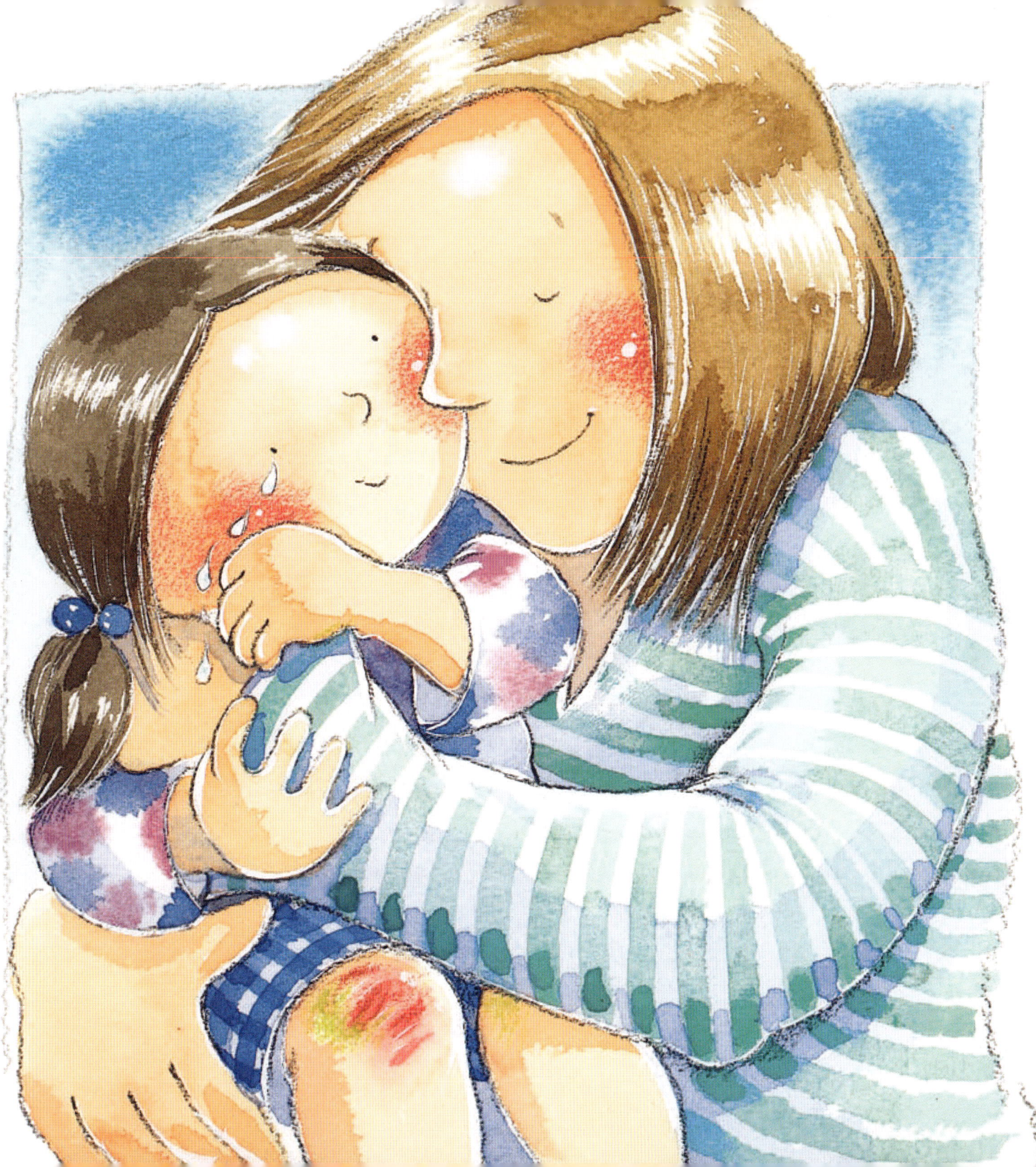

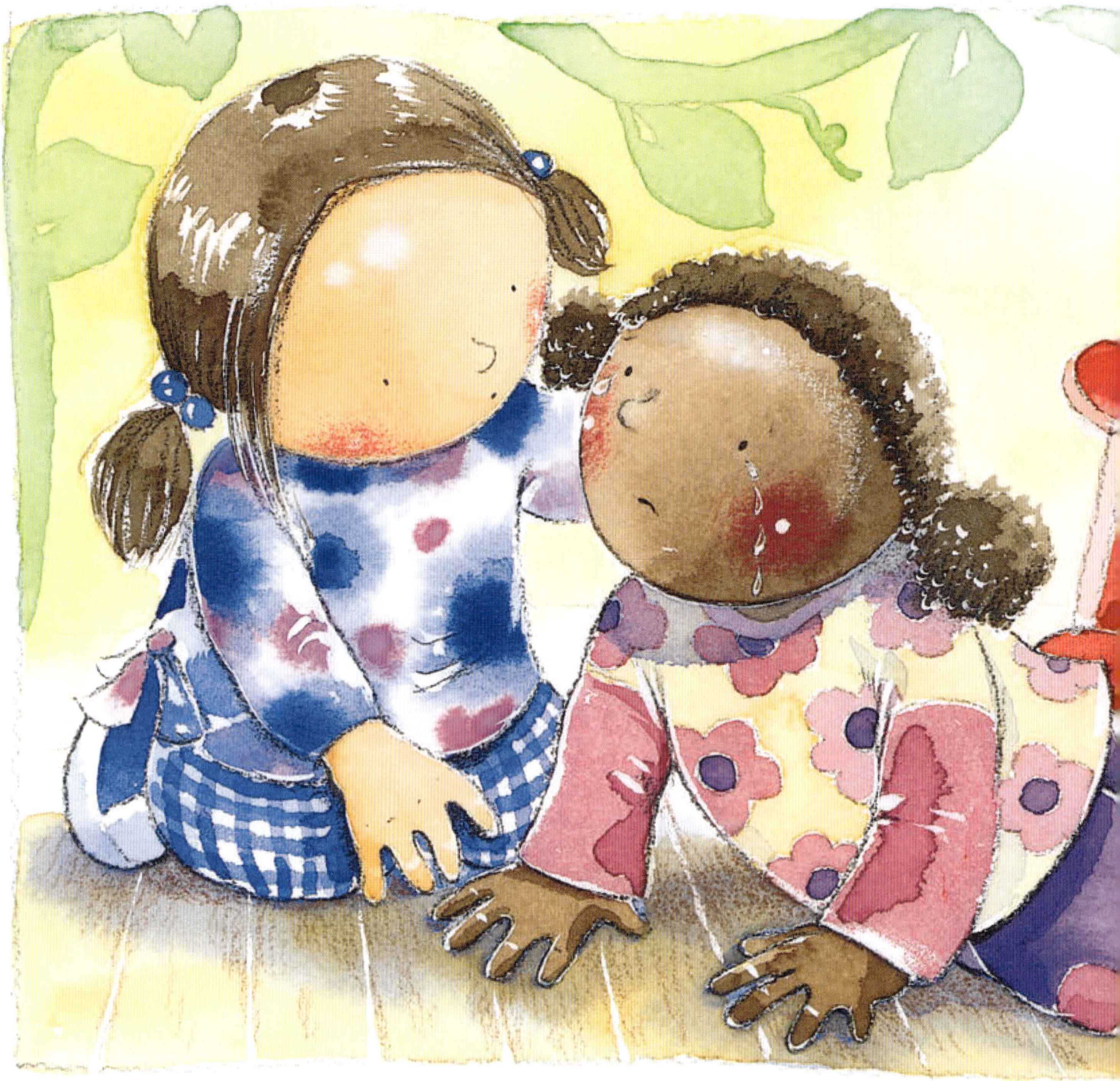

And how I can be kind too.

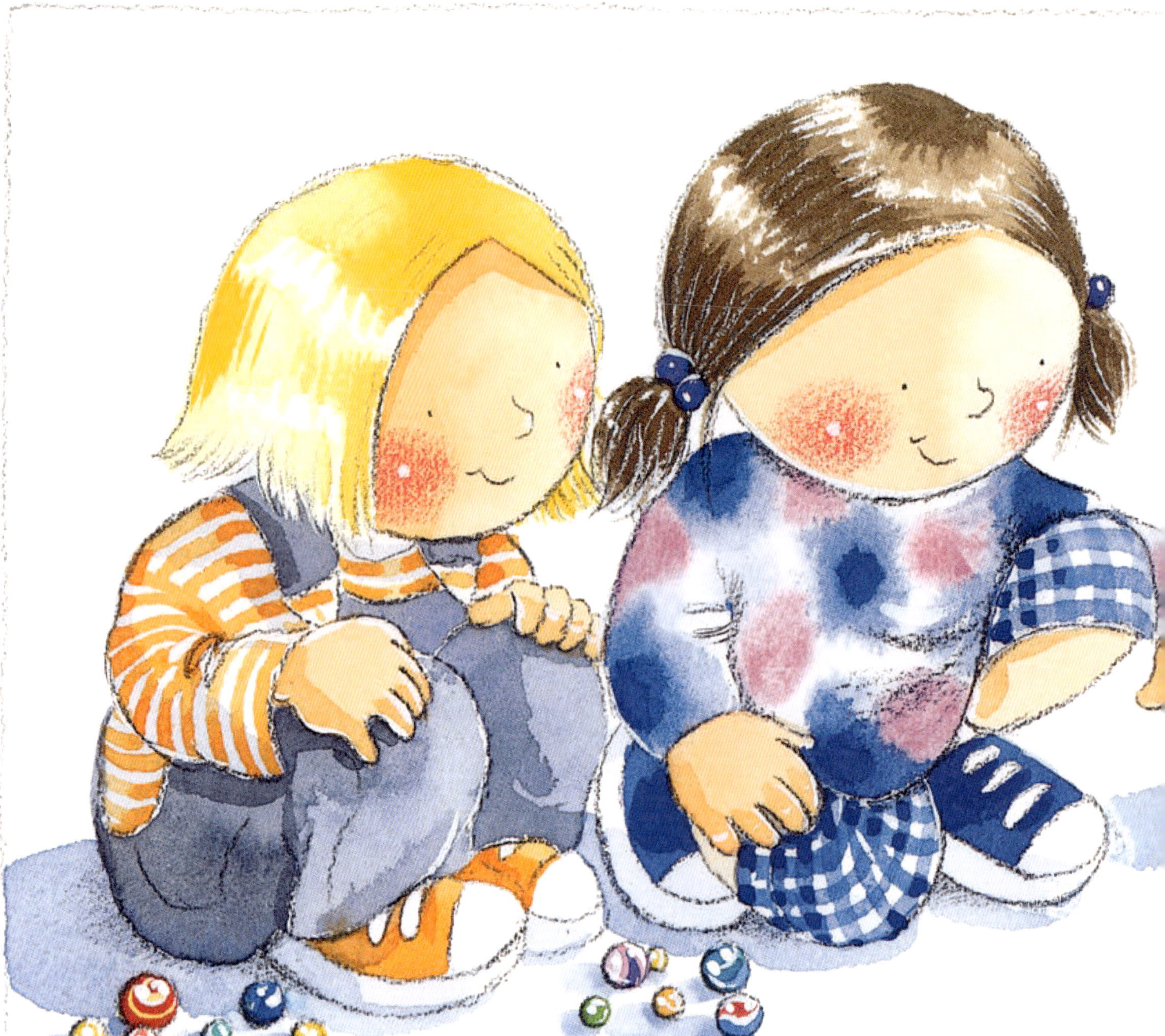

Because this does me **good.**

It's a **great** way to live.

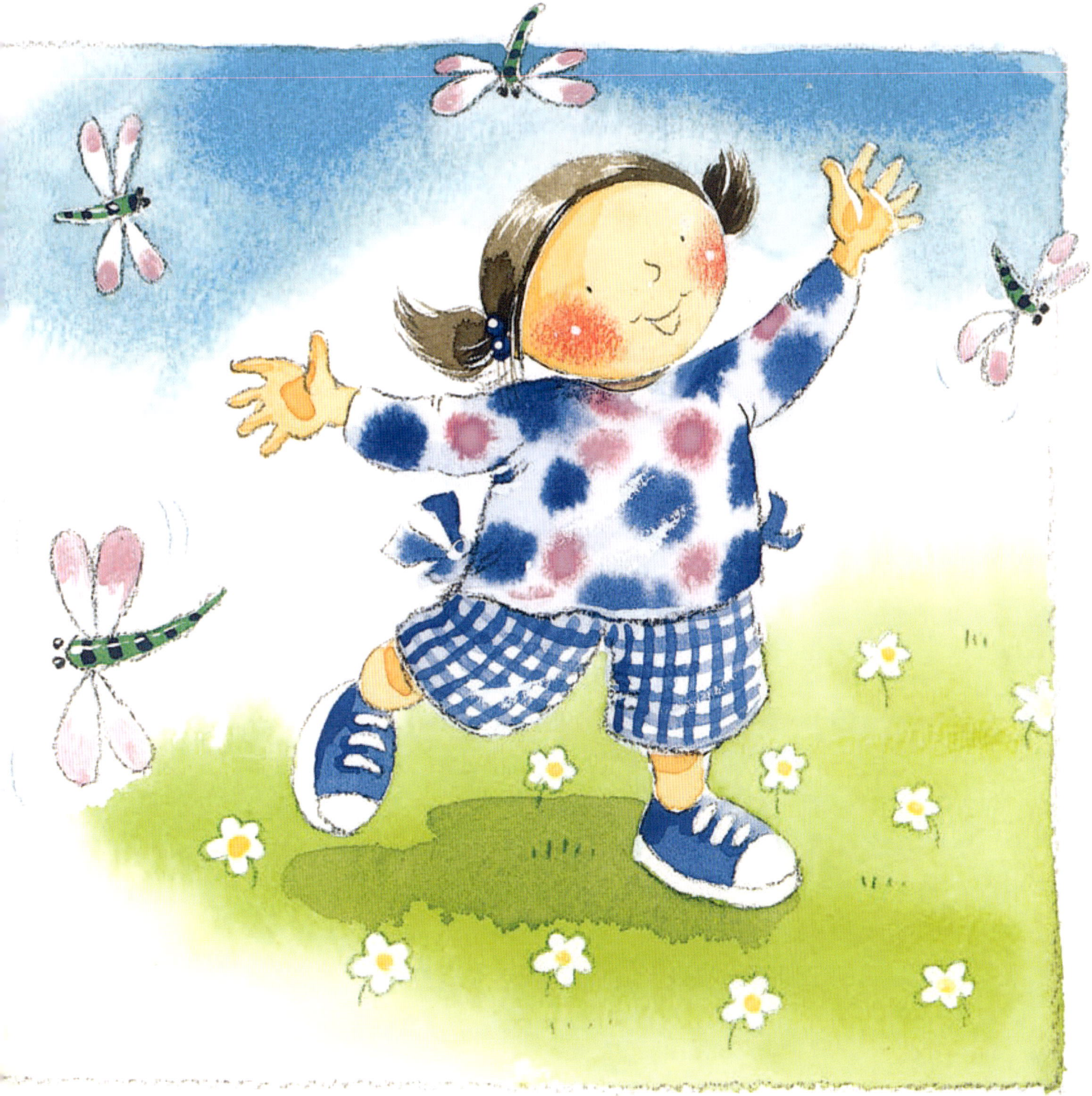

'Each day I live is written in your book.'

Always Near Me

Based on Psalm 139, The Bible

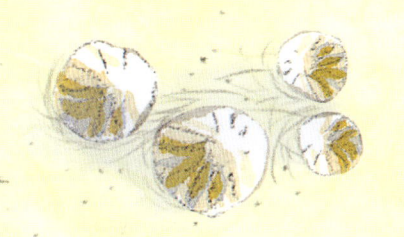

Jesus, you know me so well.

You see my heart.

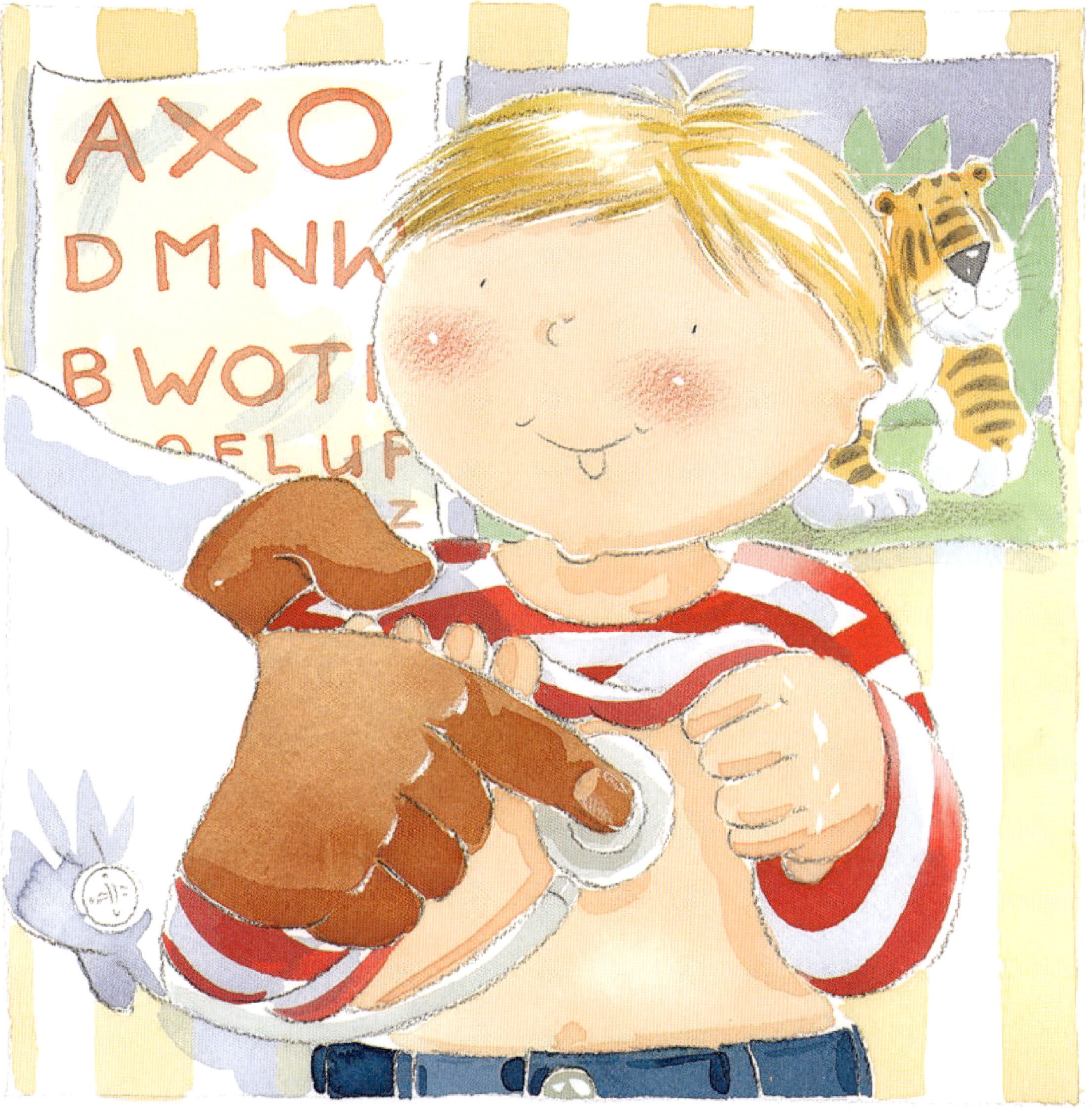
AXO
DMNK

You know when I *sit* down

and when I **stand** up.

You know my thoughts before I think them!

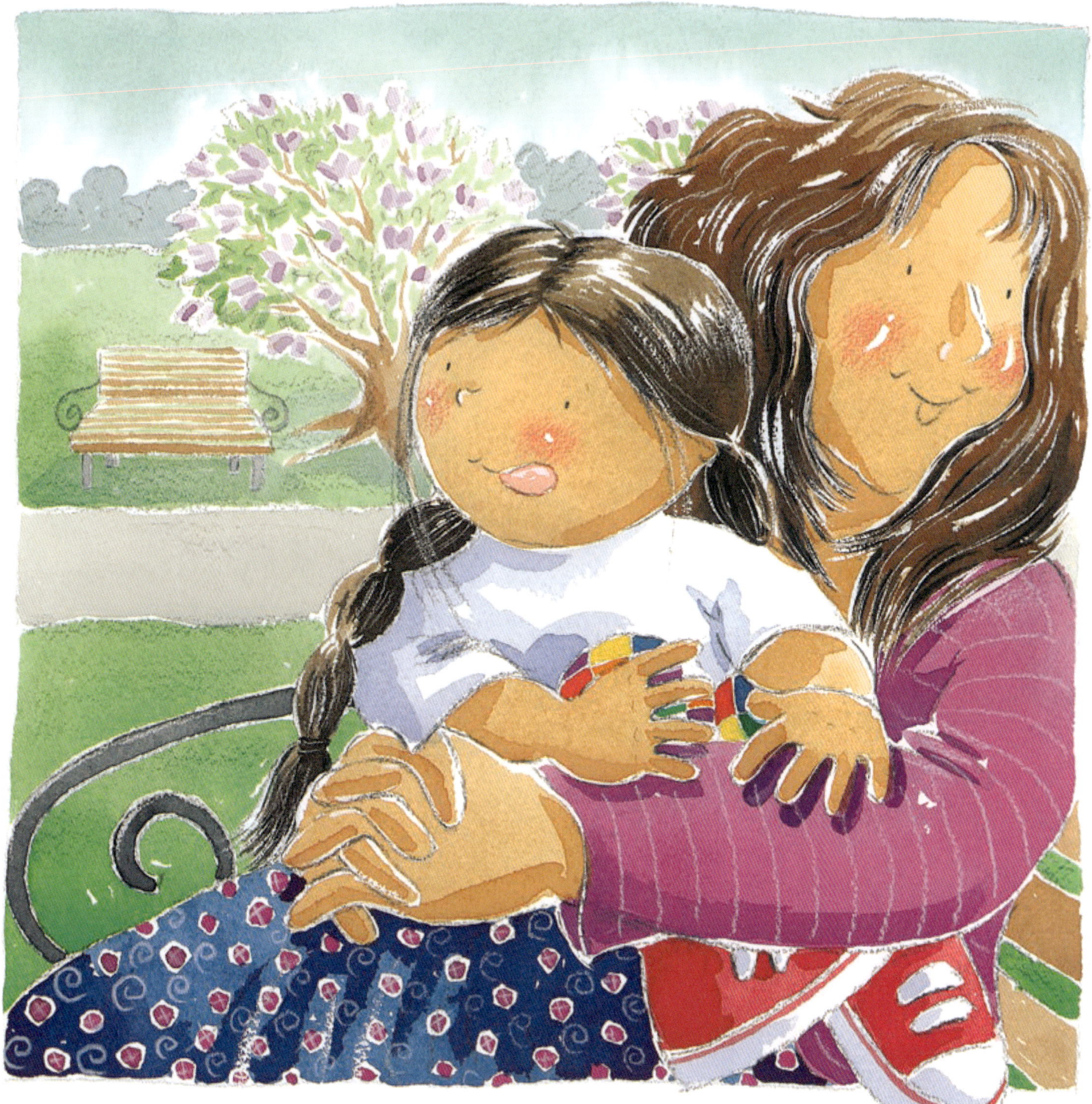

Before I get to where I'm going,

You know where I will **end up**.

Just like the wind, you are all around me.

This is very hard to understand.

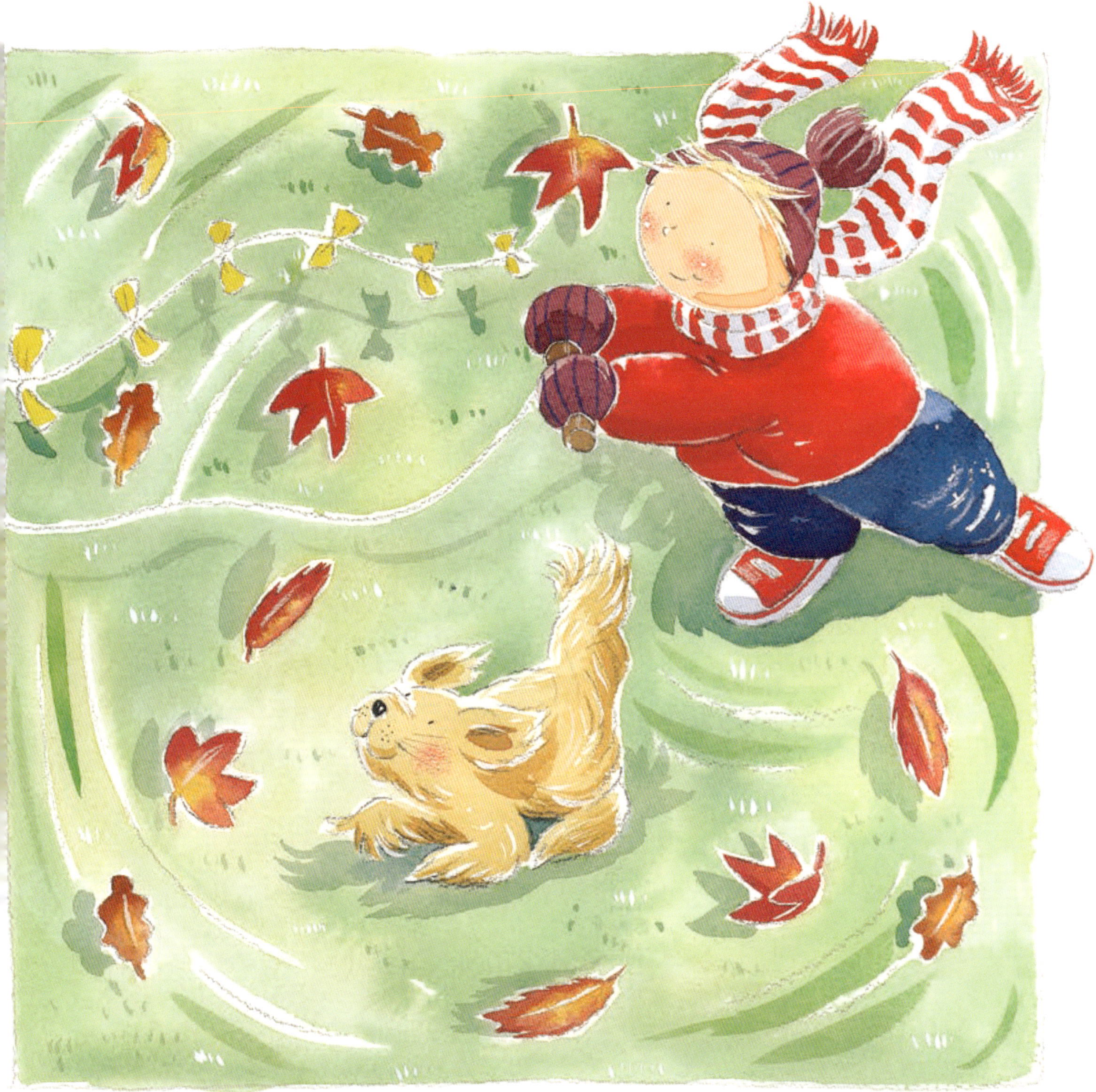

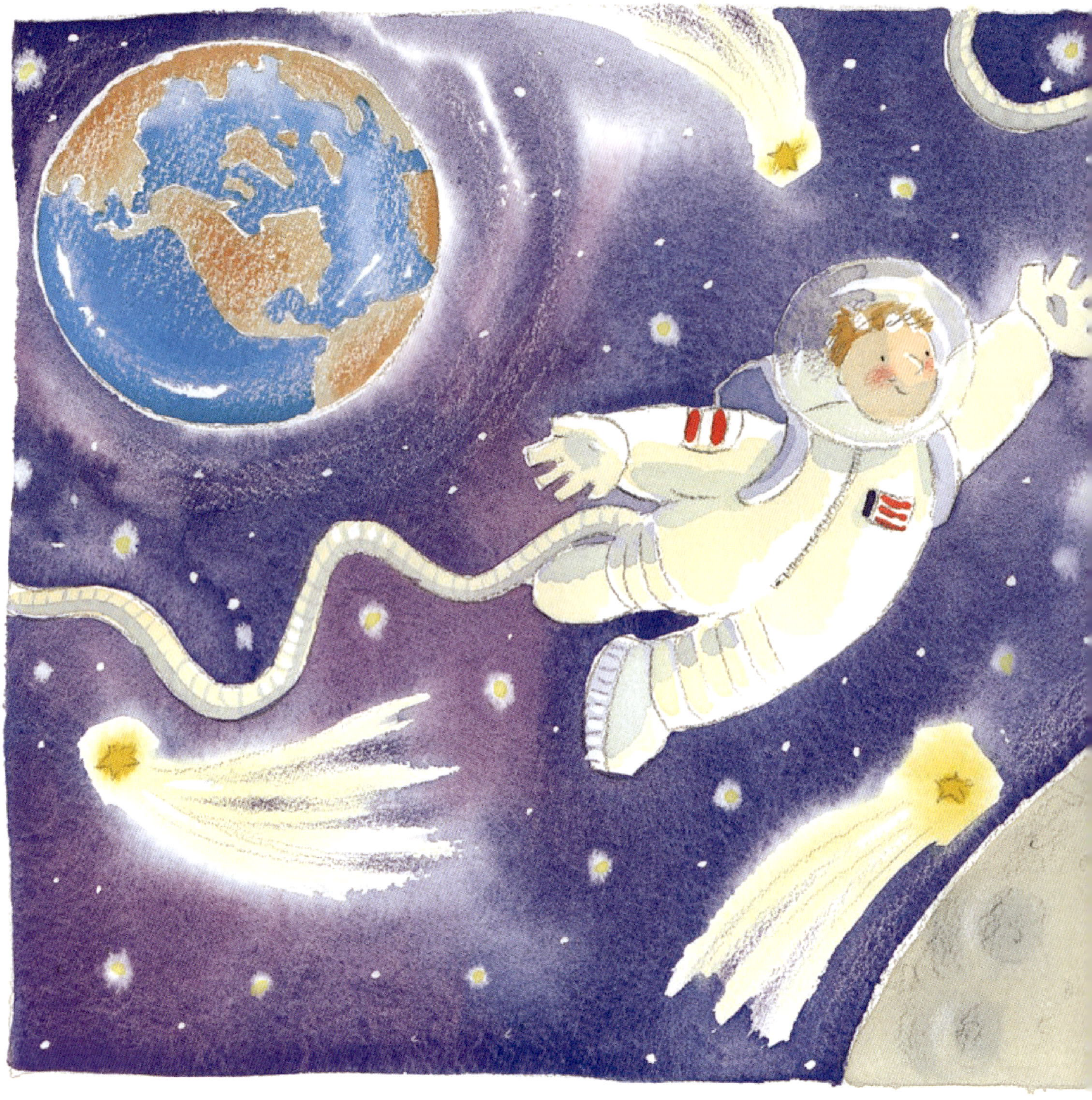

Where can I hide from you?

If I journey into space you are there.

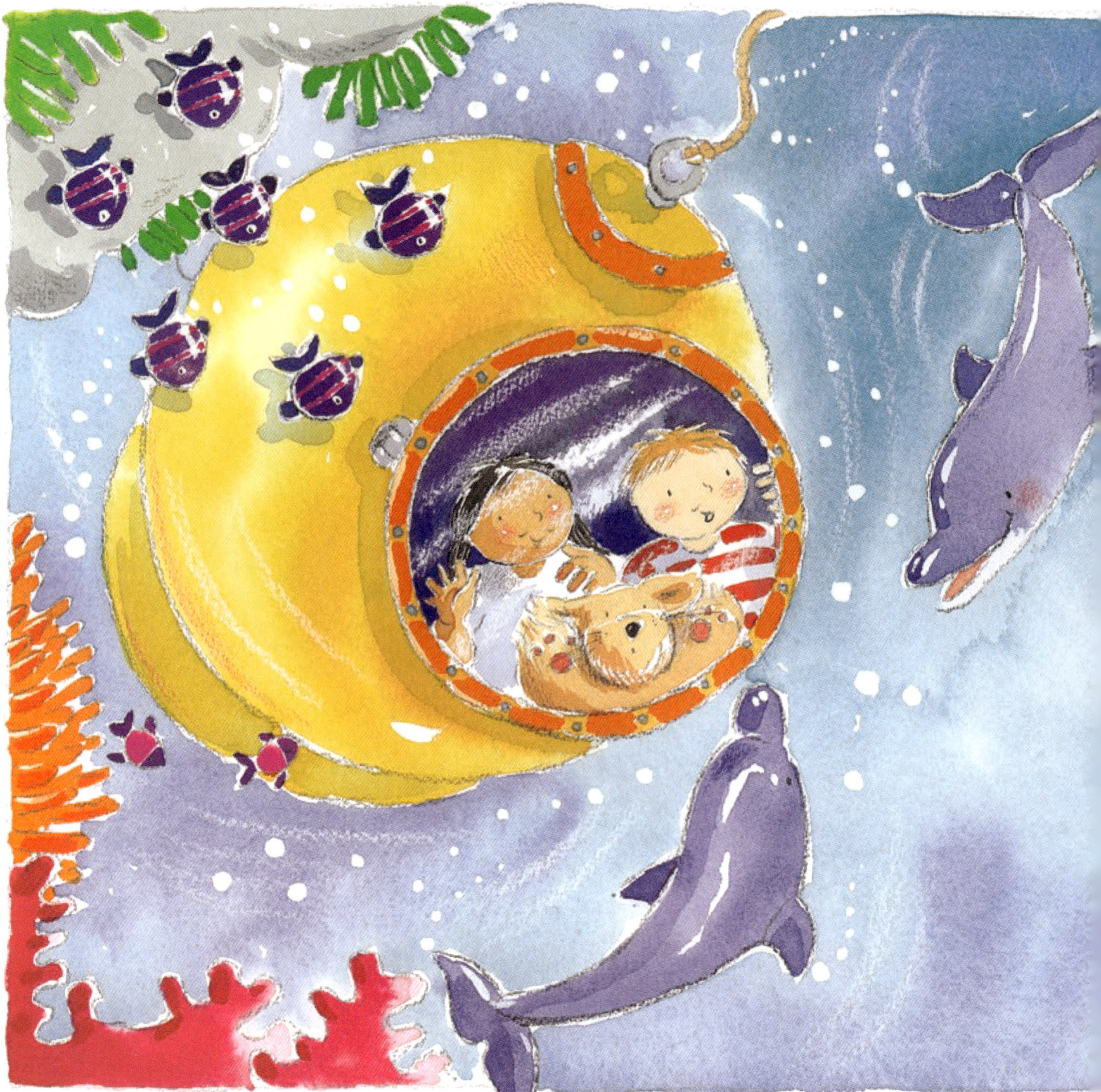

If I sink to the bottom of the sea, you will find me there too. That's because you are everywhere.

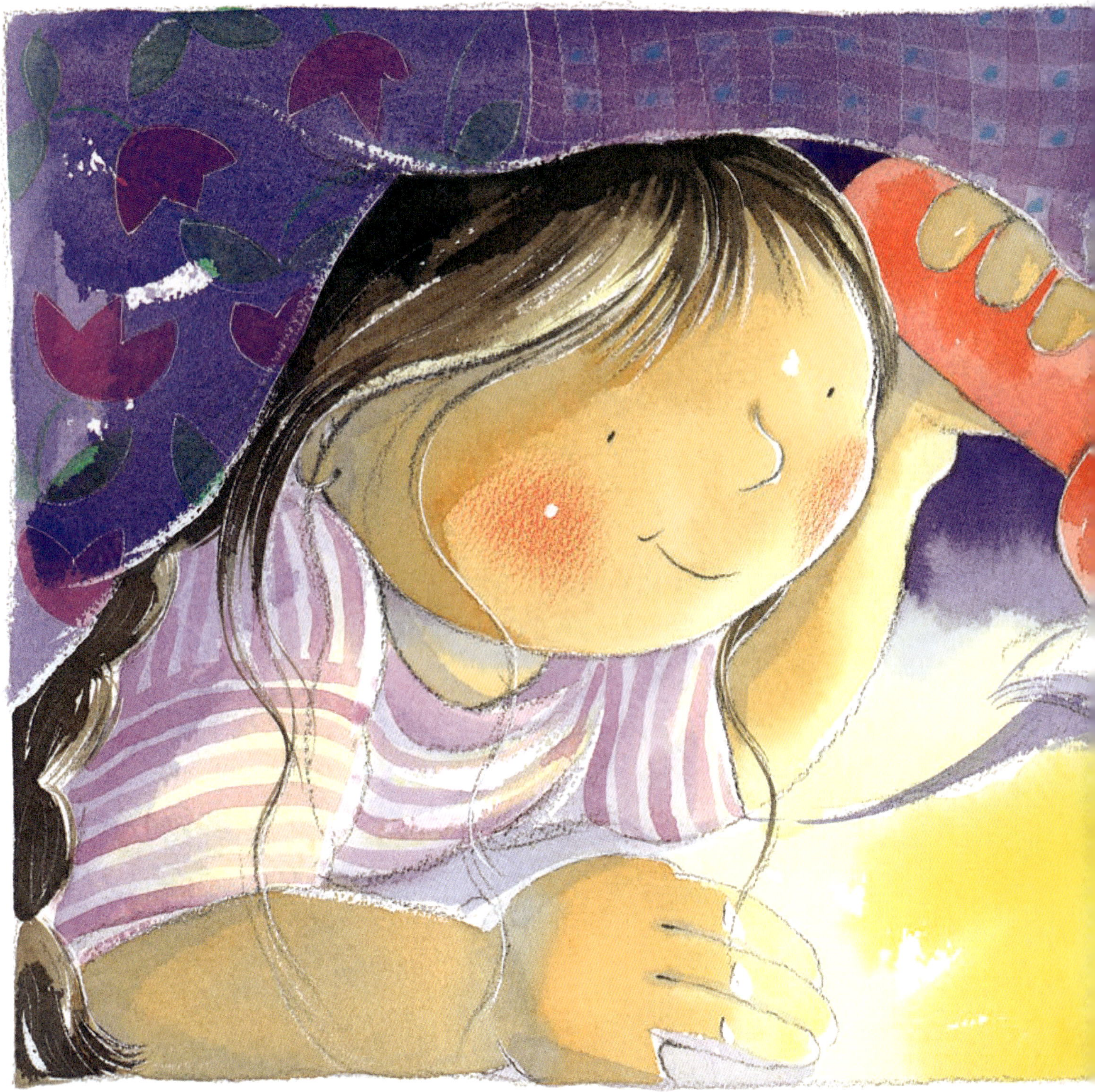

Not even the darkness can hide me. To you, daytime and night-time are just **the same.**

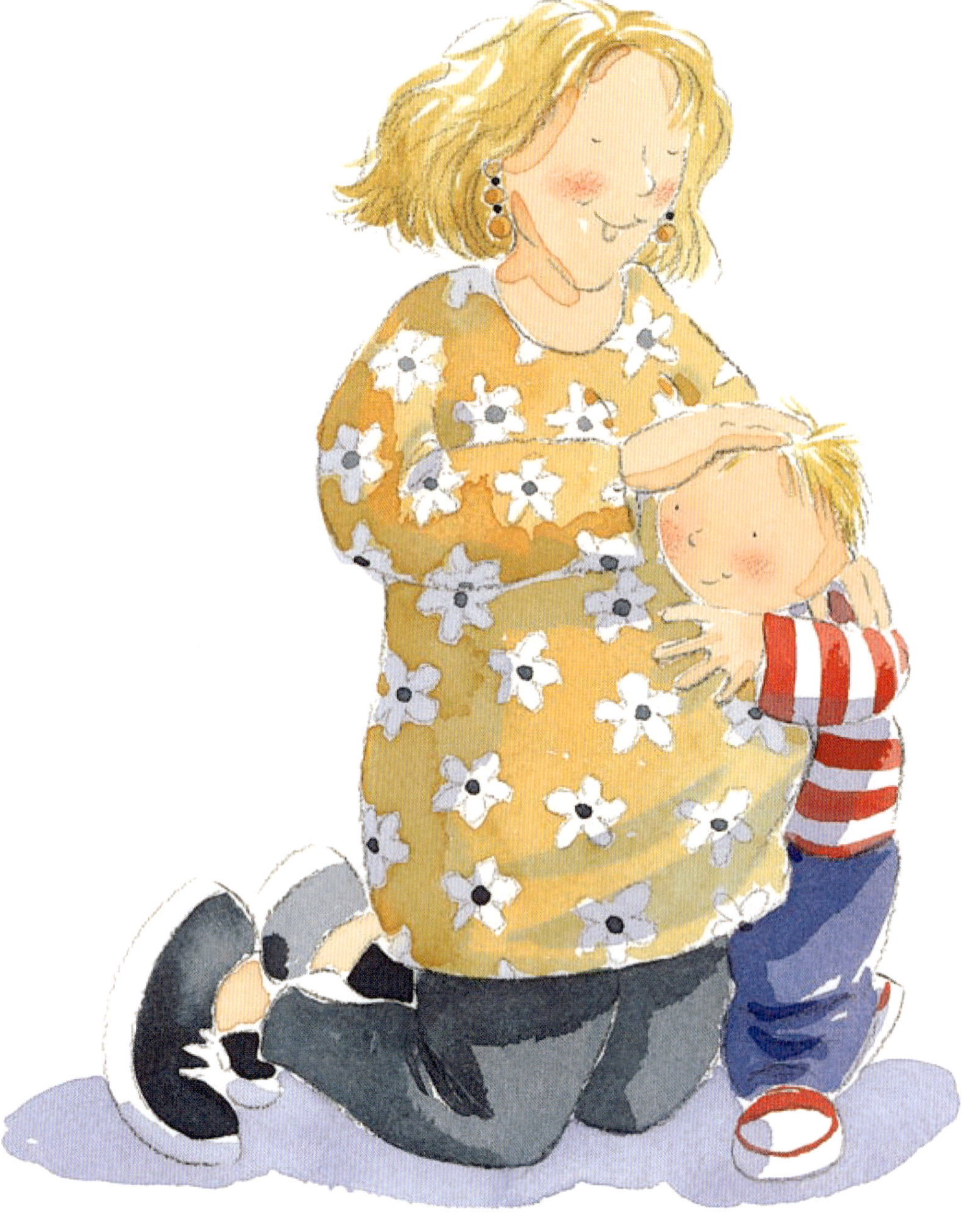

You made every part of me

and watched as I **grew** in my mummy's tummy.

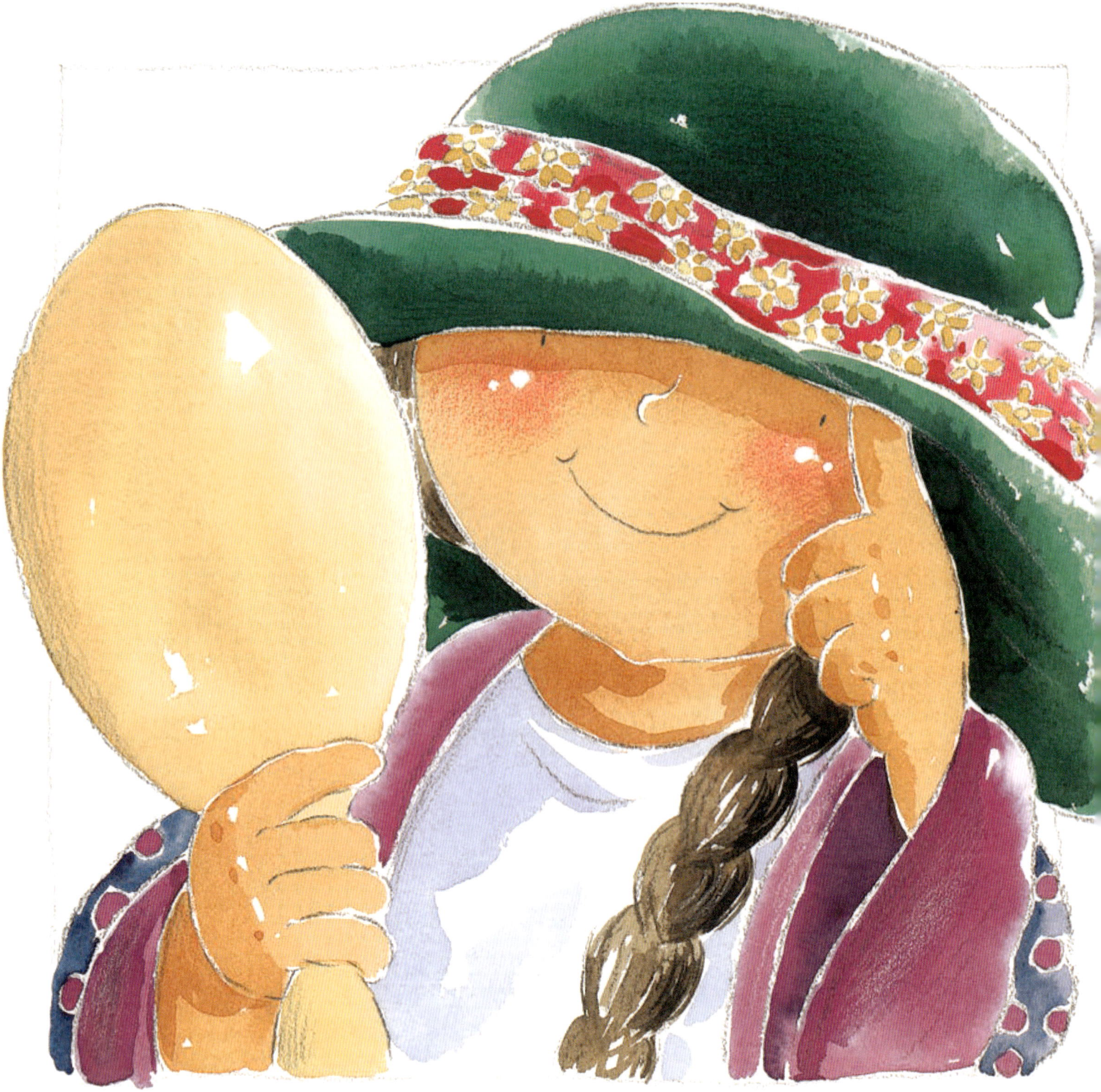

Before the world was made, you decided how I would look.

I am made wonderful in a and amazing way.

I jump for joy because of what you have done.

You will always watch over me.
Each day I live is written
in your book.

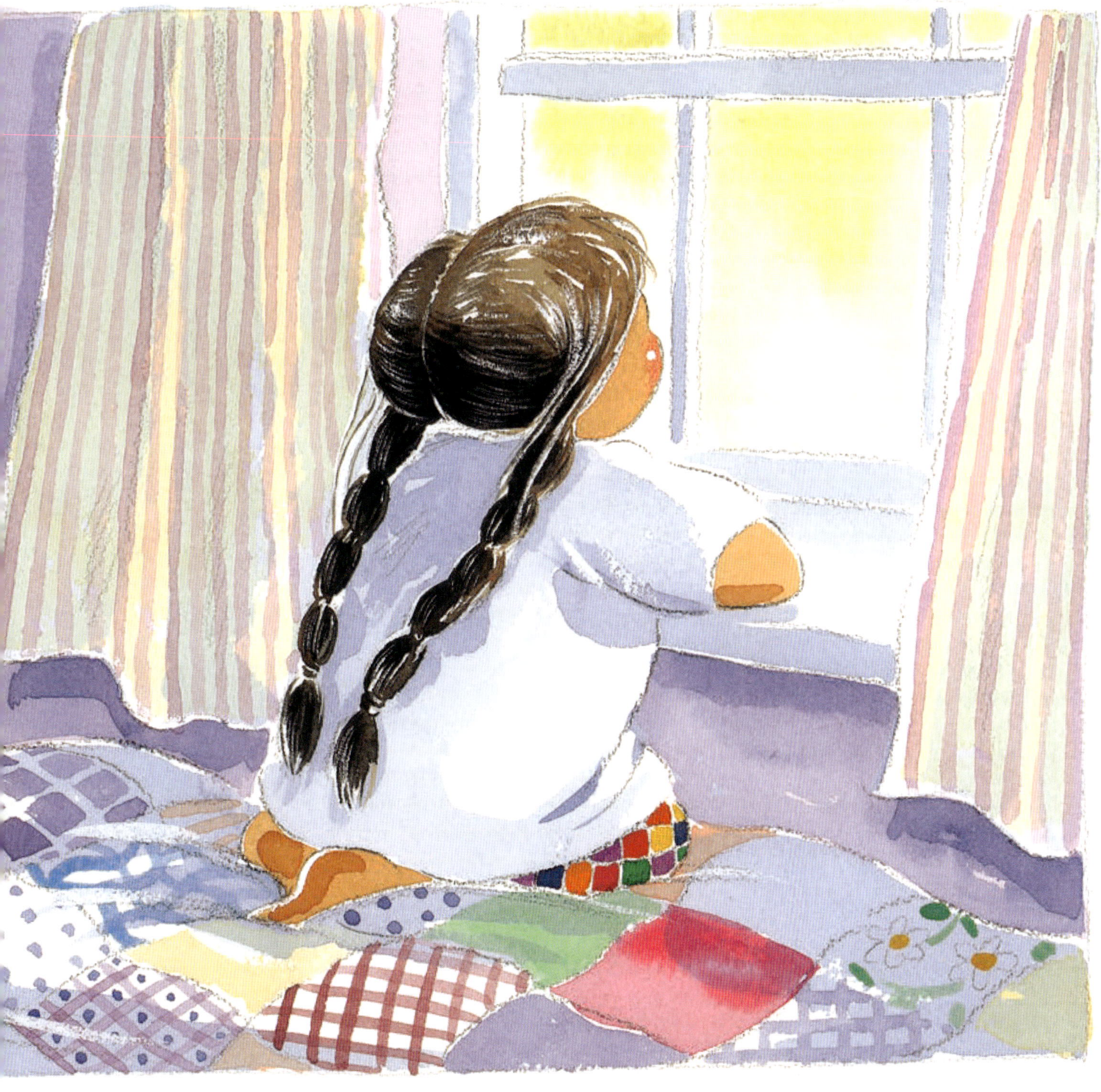

'What is
Love?'

All These Things

Based on 1 Corinthians 13, The Bible

what is LOVE?

Kisses and cuddles?

Hugs and squeezes?

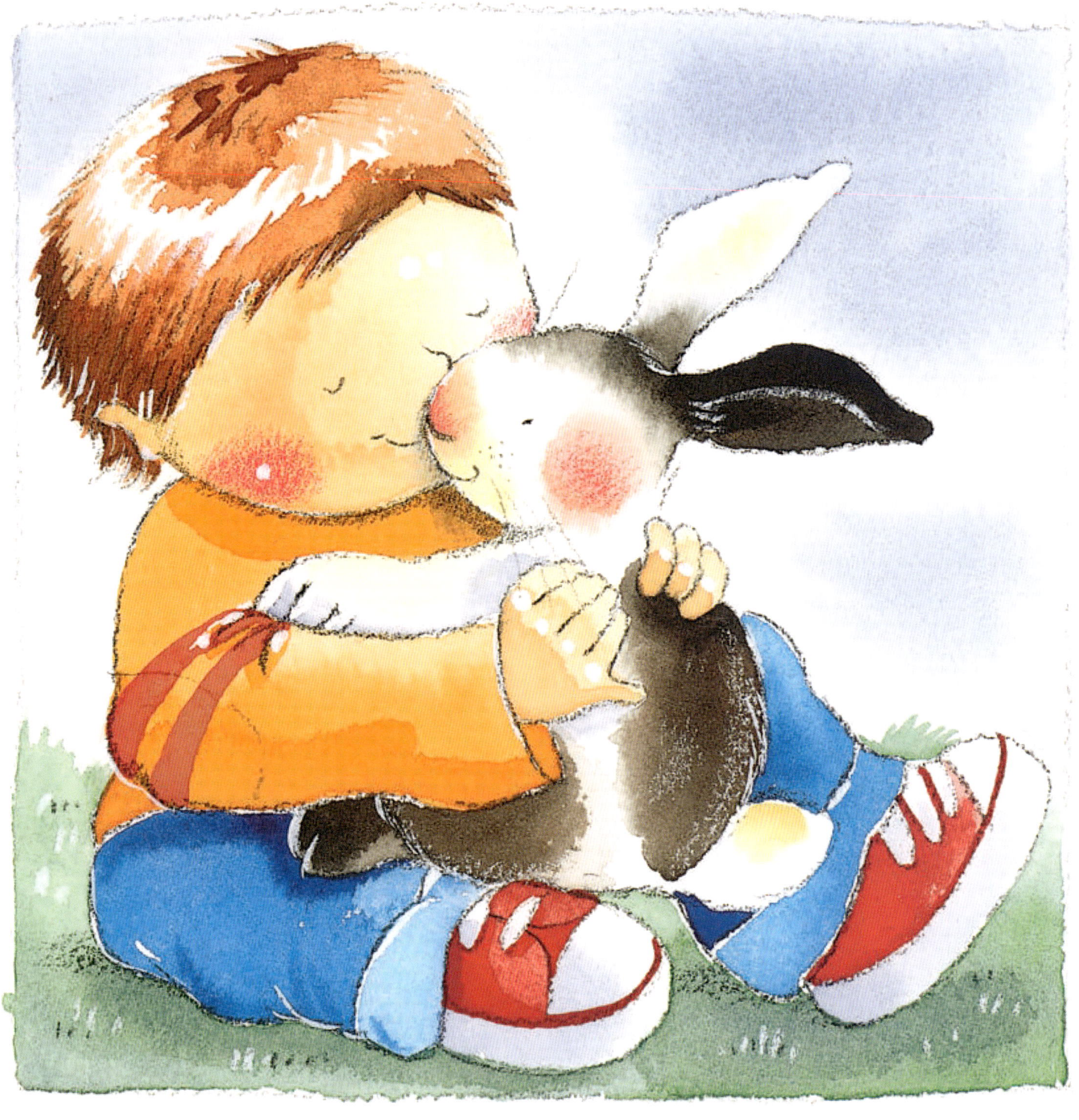

Love *is* these things.

But it's **kindness** too.

And learning to **wait** our turn.

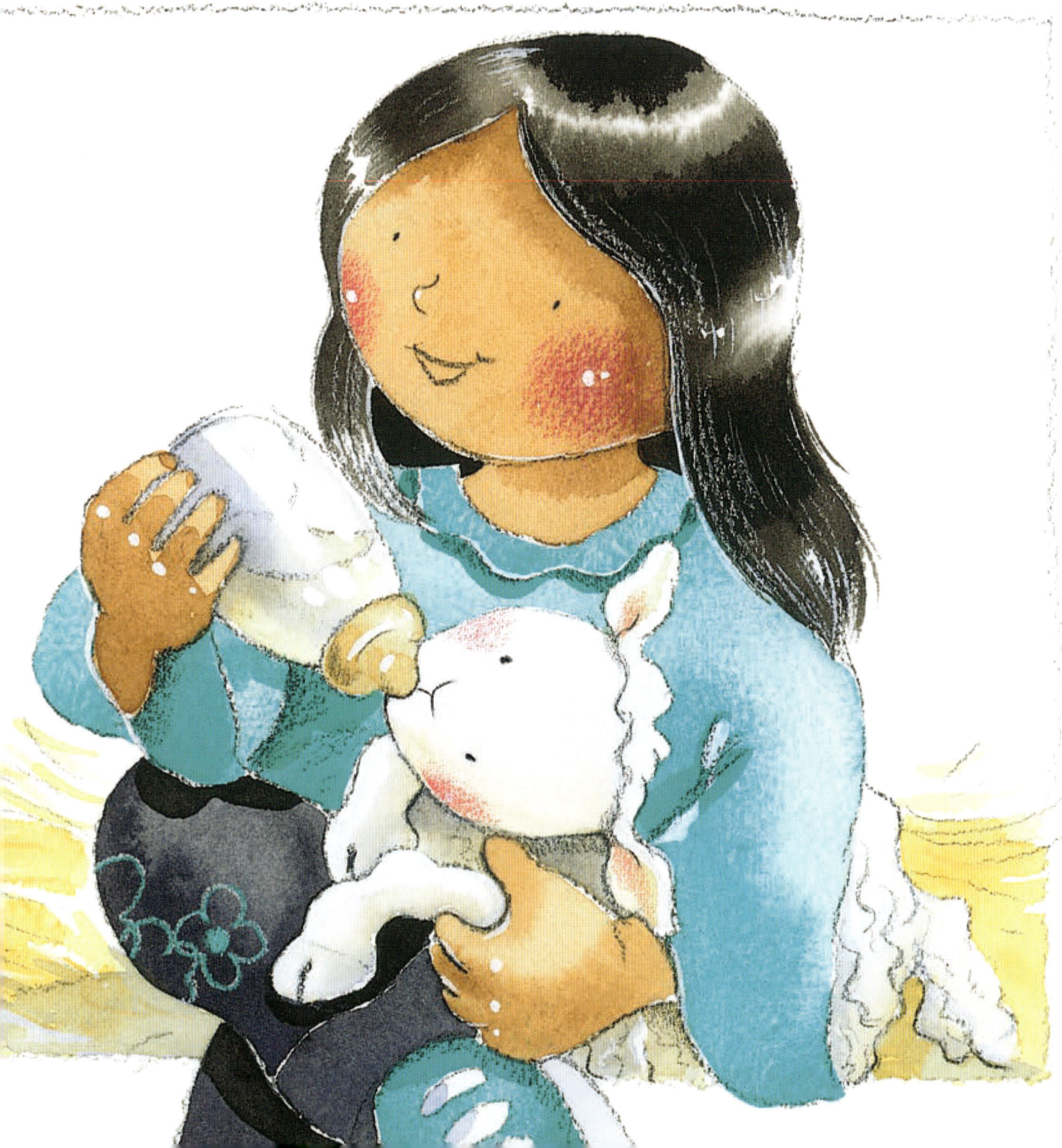

It's being **grateful**

for the things we are given.

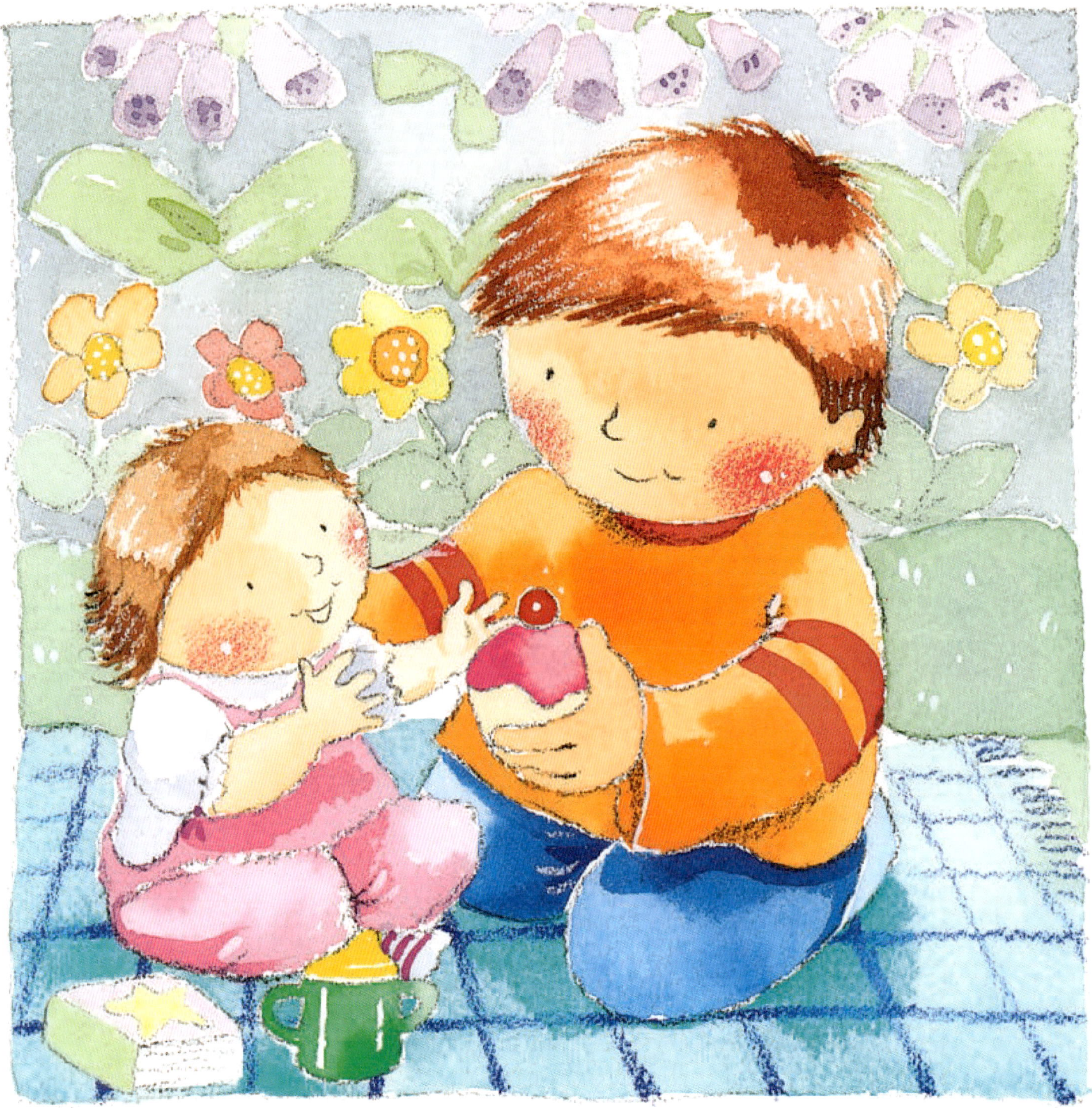

And **looking out** for those that are small.

Love is not saying
me first...

me, me, Me!

It's taking a deep breath and counting to five when we feel **cross!**

1... 2... 3... 4... 5

Love is saying 'no' to bad things.

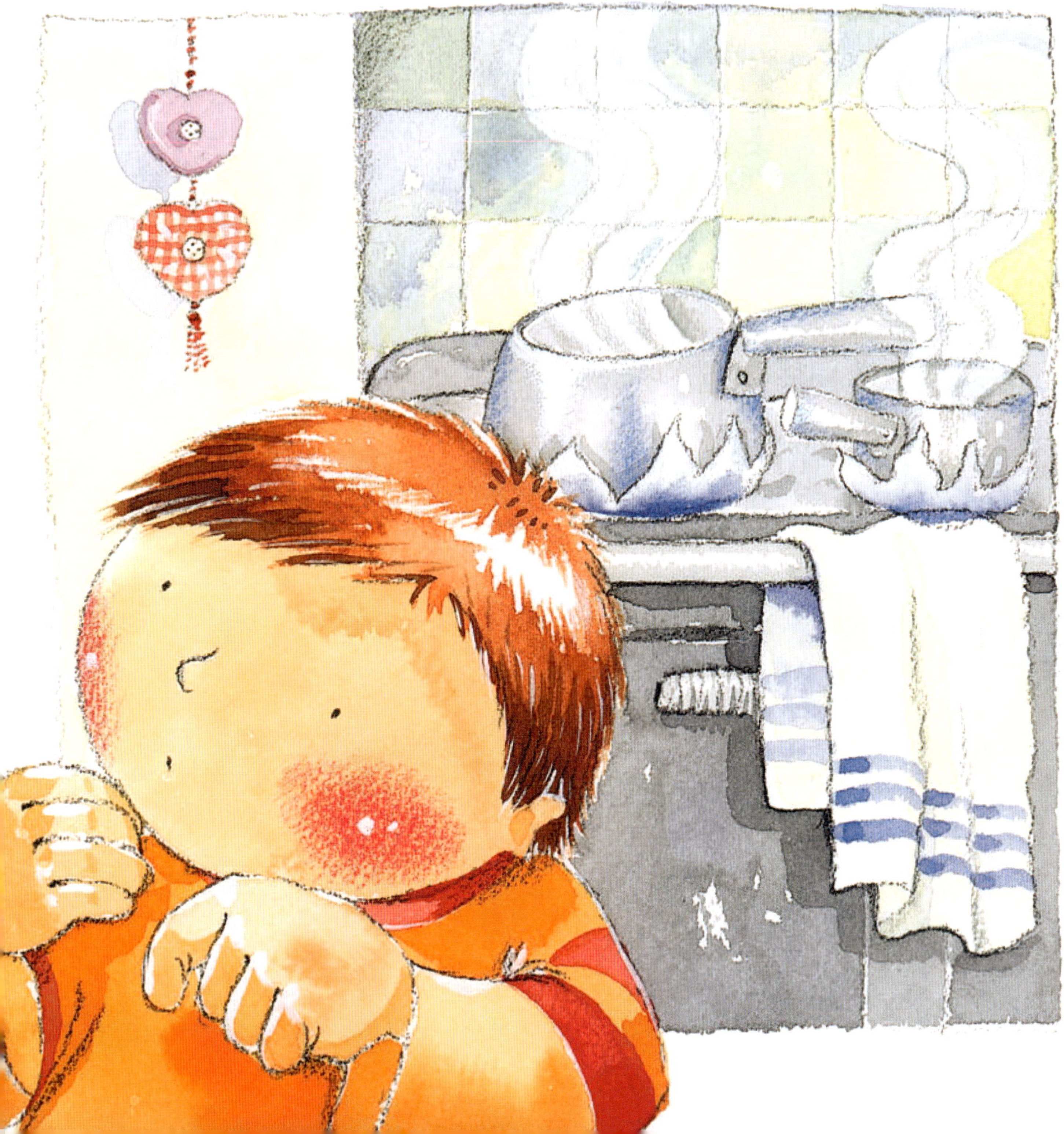

And 'yes' to good things.

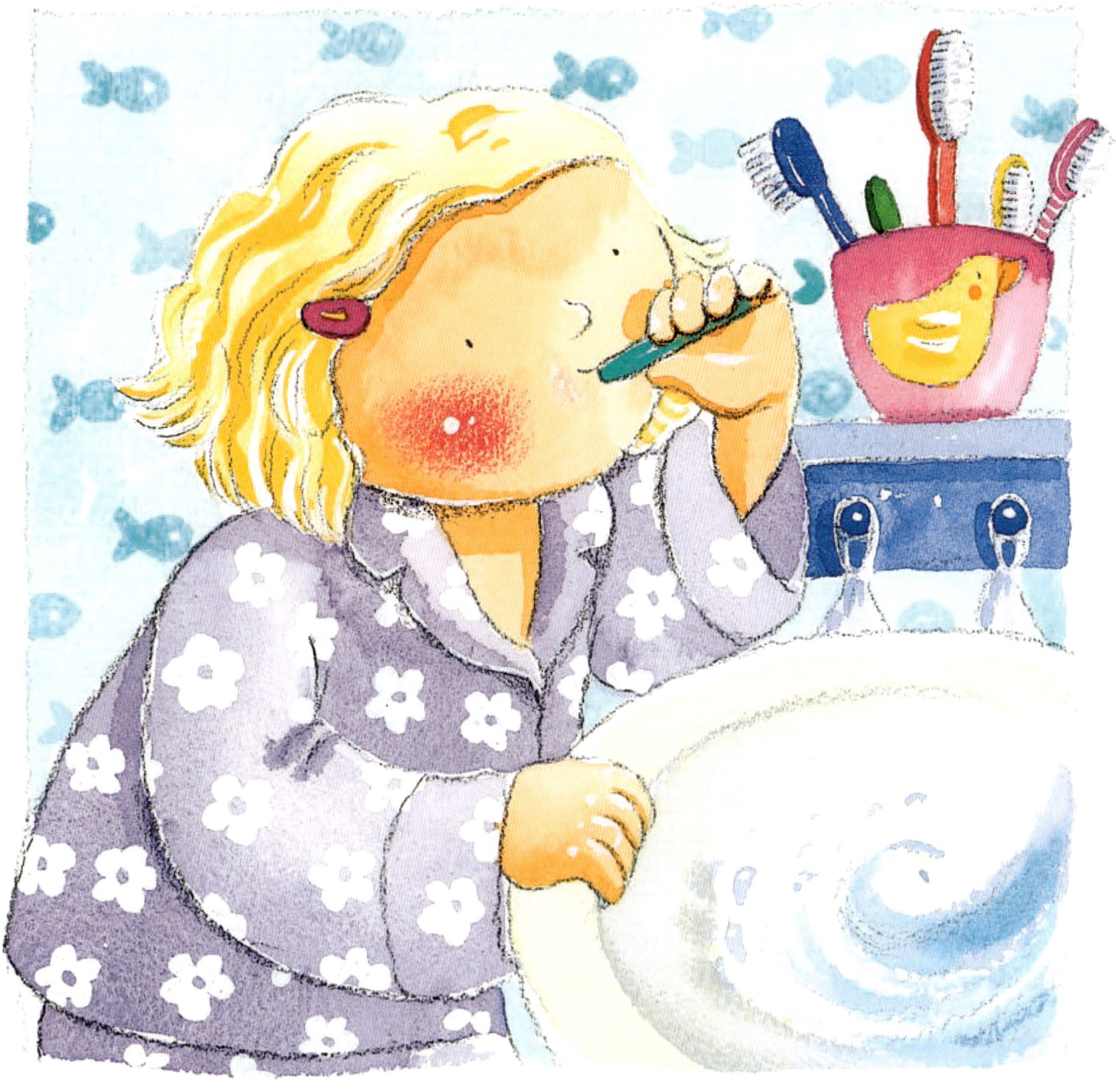

Love lets others have a go,

and hopes they will do **well**.

And when you want to give up...

Love keeps going...

Love is all these things.

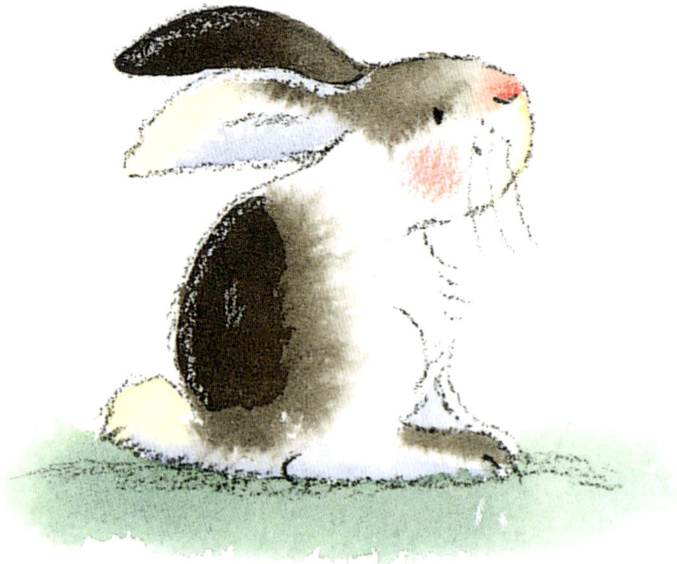

Autumn, Winter, Spring and Summer, may you be **blessed** *little* one, and know the **sunshine** of the Father's face — shining on you **always**.

Amen.

Authentic

We trust you enjoyed reading this book from Authentic. If you want to be informed of any new titles from this author and other releases you can sign up to the Authentic newsletter by scanning below:

Online:
authenticmedia.co.uk

Follow us: